TWENTY-FIFTH ANNIVERSARY SERIES

4

TRENDS IN OUTPUT AND EMPLOYMENT

Trends in Output
and Employment

GEORGE J. STIGLER
Columbia University

NATIONAL BUREAU OF ECONOMIC RESEARCH, INC.
New York
1947

Printed in the United States by
Herald Square Press, Inc.
Bound by H. Wolff, New York

Relation of the Directors to the Work and Publications
of the
National Bureau of Economic Research

1. The object of the National Bureau of Economic Research is to ascertain and to present to the public important economic facts and their interpretation in a scientific and impartial manner. The Board of Directors is charged with the responsibility of ensuring that the work of the Bureau is carried on in strict conformity with this object.

2. To this end the Board of Directors shall appoint one or more Directors of Research.

3. The Director or Directors of Research shall submit to the members of the Board, or to its Executive Committee, for their formal adoption, all specific proposals concerning researches to be instituted.

4. No report shall be published until the Director or Directors of Research shall have submitted to the Board a summary drawing attention to the character of the data and their utilization in the report, the nature and treatment of the problems involved, the main conclusions and such other information as in their opinion would serve to determine the suitability of the report for publication in accordance with the principles of the Bureau.

5. A copy of any manuscript proposed for publication shall also be submitted to each member of the Board. For each manuscript to be so submitted a special committee shall be appointed by the President, or at his designation by the Executive Director, consisting of three Directors selected as nearly as may be one from each general division of the Board. The names of the special manuscript committee shall be stated to each Director when the summary and report described in paragraph (4) are sent to him. It shall be the duty of each member of the committee to read the manuscript. If each member of the special committee signifies his approval within thirty days, the manuscript may be published. If each member of the special committee has not signified his approval within thirty days of the transmittal of the report and manuscript, the Director of Research shall then notify each member of the Board, requesting approval or disapproval of publication, and thirty additional days shall be granted for this purpose. The manuscript shall then not be published unless at least a majority of the entire Board and a two-thirds majority of those members of the Board who shall have voted on the proposal within the time fixed for the receipt of votes on the publication proposed shall have approved.

6. No manuscript may be published, though approved by each member of the special committee, until forty-five days have elapsed from the transmittal of the summary and report. The interval is allowed for the receipt of any memorandum of dissent or reservation, together with a brief statement of his reasons, that any member may wish to express; and such memorandum of dissent or reservation shall be published with the manuscript if he so desires. Publication does not, however, imply that each member of the Board has read the manuscript, or that either members of the Board in general, or of the special committee, have passed upon its validity in every detail.

7. A copy of this resolution shall, unless otherwise determined by the Board, be printed in each copy of every National Bureau book.

(Resolution adopted October 25, 1926 and revised February 6, 1933 and February 24, 1941)

CONTENTS

Acknowledgments

This report is the eleventh in a series dealing with changes in production, employment, and productivity in American industry since the beginning of the twentieth century. The studies upon which it is based were made possible by funds granted by The Maurice and Laura Falk Foundation of Pittsburgh. The Falk Foundation is not, however, the author, publisher, or proprietor of this publication, and is not to be understood as approving or disapproving by virtue of its grant any of the statements made or views expressed therein.

Helpful suggestions and criticisms were received from E. Wight Bakke and Milton Friedman; also from members of the Research Staff of the National Bureau of Economic Research, particularly Arthur F. Burns and Solomon Fabricant. Miss Martha Anderson improved the manuscript with her editorial revision, and H. Irving Forman drew the charts.

ix

Introduction

The economic problem is commonly defined as the efficient allocation of productive resources among competing ends. For the economy as a whole, the economic problem is to satisfy our wants as fully as possible with the limited amounts of resources (including knowledge) at our disposal. The success with which the problem is solved by our economic system must be appraised, relative to the past, to other countries, or even to our hopes, by the amount and growth of output, by the economy's ability to produce a given output with decreasing amounts of our scarce resources, and by its ability to employ all our available resources.

Nor are we concerned only with aggregates of outputs and inputs. There is a subsidiary economic problem for every type of output, whether we classify it broadly as manufactures or more narrowly as wheat bread. Is efficiency growing fast or slowly in filling what are usually viewed as basic needs—food, clothing, and shelter? Are we employing more or less of our resources in providing through investment for a larger future output, in supplying personal services, in maintaining governmental activities?

Comprehensive and continuous information on the size and composition of the outputs of goods and the inputs of resources is necessary to answer these and many other significant questions. Our present information cannot be said to be entirely satisfactory. Data on output and labor input are relatively adequate only for the period since about 1900, and then for merely a portion of the economy. In other sectors, such as personal services and government, aside from limitations of data there are serious conceptual problems in measuring output—to be discussed later. Yet the studies of output, employment, and output per worker so far completed at the National Bureau provide the most comprehensive informa-

1

tion yet assembled on trends during a fairly long period, and they are our main source in this essay.*

The findings illuminate a multitude of inquiries, but we confine discussion to a summary of how they bear on three important questions:

1 How has the magnitude and composition of output—the end product of economic activity—varied over time?

2 How has labor—the most important of our scarce resources —changed in amount, composition, and distribution?

3 What changes have taken place over time in the efficiency with which labor is utilized?

A synopsis of the broad answers to these questions will first be given. Against this general background, I shall then discuss more detailed findings of the studies.

*The volumes already published are:

The Output of Manufacturing Industries, 1899-1937 (1940) and *Employment in Manufacturing, 1899-1939* (1942), both by Solomon Fabricant; *American Agriculture, 1899-1939* (1942), by Harold Barger and H. H. Landsberg; *The Mining Industries, 1899-1939* (1944), by Harold Barger and S. H. Schurr; *Output and Productivity in the Electric and Gas Utilities, 1899-1942* (1946), by J. M. Gould.

In addition the following *Occasional Papers* have been published: Manufacturing Output, 1929-1937 (1940), The Relation between Factory Employment and Output since 1899 (1941), Productivity of Labor in Peace and War (1942), and Labor Savings in American Industry, 1899-1939 (1945) by Solomon Fabricant; Domestic Servants in the United States, 1900-1940 (1946), by George J. Stigler.

An unpublished study of railroad transportation by Harold Barger was also used.

A Preview of the General Findings

The National Bureau studies of output and employment cover four-tenths of the American economy, if coverage is measured by national income originating in agriculture, manufacturing, mining, gas and electric utilities, and steam railroads. These industries employed two-thirds of the nation's labor force in 1899, and slightly less than half in 1939. They produced about nine-tenths of the output of the commodity-producing industries and one-tenth of the output of the service-producing industries.

Indexes of output, employment, and output per worker for the six industries combined are as follows:

	1899	1909	1919	1929	1939
Output	100	146	195	283	289
Employment	100	129	153	150	130
Output per worker	100	113	127	189	222

Perhaps the outstanding finding is that output nearly tripled during the four decades. We should like to take into numerical account also two important developments our index of output does not reflect. On the one hand, large improvements in quality of product appear to have occurred, and on this score the index has a downward bias. On the other hand, production within the household declined substantially, and on this score the index has an upward bias. If, as we believe, the former tendency has been definitely the stronger, output may have considerably more than tripled between 1899 and 1939.

Employment in the six industries was only a third larger in 1939 than in 1899, and even this moderate increase was completely offset by the decline in working hours. That is, while output tripled, man-hours of employment remained the same.

Until 1929, the growth of output was large—3.5 percent a

year on the average; it then fell sharply, and a decade later recovered only to the 1929 level. Employment had already reached its peak by 1919—in our decennial index—but again the effect of the protracted depression of the 'thirties is plain: employment fell more than an eighth and there was widespread involuntary shortening of the work week. Of the three indexes, output per worker alone does not show a break in trend: the advance in the fourth decade was larger than in two of the three preceding decades.

The major shift in the composition of output was between agriculture and manufacturing. Agriculture's share of the output of the six industries (measured by 'value-added') fell from 31 percent in 1899 to 16 percent in 1939, and manufacture's share rose from 49 to 62 percent. A corresponding shift took place in the labor force: agriculture had 56 percent of the labor force of the six industries in 1900 and 37 percent in 1940; meanwhile manufacture's percentage rose from 32 to 49.

When we examine the outputs of consumer goods, we find —as we expect—growth in the relative importance of consumer durables. But we also find, and this is rather surprising, that the output of food and clothing appears to have increased about as rapidly as the output of all commodities. The latter growth reflects the shift to more expensive commodities, the additional processing of food before it leaves manufacturing, and the decline in the amount of food grown and consumed on farms.

Changes in output per worker in a group of 32 manufacturing industries are analyzed in some detail. The change in output per worker (and also in output per man-hour) appears to be very erratic during short periods—ranging from —3.2 percent per year (in 1931-33) to 5.4 percent per year (in 1937-39) within a single decade—despite the relative steadiness of the long-term growth. Nor do individual industries maintain stable positions with respect to the group: the rank of an industry in the hierarchy of increases in output per worker (or per man-hour) fluctuates widely from period to period.

Changes in output per worker are not to be confused with changes in efficiency—changes in output per unit of all productive services—although over long periods we expect a fair correspondence between them. A very tentative measure of changes in efficiency confirms the impression of great technological advance obtained from data on output per worker, but suggests that changes in output per worker is an unreliable guide to changes in the efficiency of industries where labor costs are a relatively small part of total costs.

CHAPTER 1

Trends in Output

So far studies have been completed of the outputs of six broad industrial groups containing scores of individual industries that produce a multitude of products. To obtain a broad view of the findings, we begin by analyzing the place of the six industry groups in the economy and proceed to estimate their aggregate output. The effects on aggregate output of changes in quality of product and the transfer of activities from the household to the market, and the problems of the measurement of output in the chief unexplored section of the economy—the service industries—are then discussed. Finally, we turn to changes in the composition of the output of the six industry groups and investigate their implications for several interesting questions concerning the theory and facts of economic development.

Total Output

The net output of the economy consists of the production of commodities and services for current consumption plus the addition made to stocks of goods and resources that permits larger consumption in the future. This flow of output is the national income; so for a broad view of the change over time in the economy's net output we look at the movements of national income.

There are, however, two tall obstacles to the use of national income figures to measure net output in 'real' terms. The first is that national income is a series of aggregate money flows, whereas our interest is in the outputs of goods and services somehow divorced, or at least amicably separated, from fluctuations in the value of the dollar. This obstacle is surmounted by deflating national income in current dollars by one or a series of price indexes. These price indexes, however, are extremely difficult to construct on a basis appropriate to the aim of measuring real national income. The necessary information on retail prices is scanty even for the fairly recent past. And even if we had the data, we would still have to surmount the difficulty that confronts all attempts to measure 'real' changes, the so-called index-number problem: we wish to achieve the inconsistent objectives of giving due weight to the relative importance of various commodities at any one time and yet, although this relative importance often changes rapidly, of maintaining comparability through time.

The second difficulty, for our purposes, in the use of national income figures is that prior to 1919 they are primarily series on physical output measured in current or constant prices. With the important exception of services (which are deflated by the prices of commodities), all components of Kuznets' series on national product (which goes back to 1869) rest largely upon the same underlying data as the output studies. Differences between the National Bureau series on physical output and the corresponding segments of real national income are therefore due in considerable part to differences in the way current prices are deflated. For this reason, and because of the considerable uncertainty surrounding estimates of national income in the earlier years,[1] we do not discuss the trend of national income since 1900. Kuznets' findings on the long-term movements of national product are summarized in the first volume of this series: *National Income: A Summary of Findings.*

We may use the national income data since 1919, when they are independent in source and detailed in composition, to get a general idea of the comprehensiveness of the productivity studies already published. About 40 percent of national income in the two interwar decades has been covered

[1]The uncertainty is illustrated, but not measured, by the fact that R. F. Martin's estimates for average national product in 1889-98 are about 12 percent larger than Kuznets', although the underlying methods and data are by no means independent. See Kuznets, *National Product since 1869* (National Bureau of Economic Research, 1946), p. 86; Martin, *National Income in the United States, 1799-1938* (National Industrial Conference Board, 1939).

in the productivity studies (see Table 1). The coverage is much greater for commodity- than for service-producing industries: indexes of output have been compiled for 90 percent of the industries (measured by their contribution to national income) producing physical commodities, but for only 11 percent of the industries that provide services.

TABLE 1

Scope of National Bureau Studies of Productivity, Measured by the Average Percentage of National Income Originating in Six Industries, 1919-1938

Industries Covered by Indexes of Output	PERCENTAGE OF NATIONAL INCOME
Commodity-producing	
Manufacturing	21.0
Agriculture	9.6
Mining	2.2
Service-producing	
Electric Light and Power	1.4
Manufactured and Natural Gas	.2
Steam Railroads	5.4
Total	39.8
Industries not Covered	
Commodity-producing	
Construction	3.8
Service-producing	
Other Public Utilities	2.8
Trade	13.5
Finance	11.9
Service	12.6
Government	11.6
Miscellaneous	4.0
Total	60.2

SOURCE: Simon Kuznets, *National Income and Its Composition* (National Bureau of Economic Research, 1941), I, 166.

Inadequacies of data on weights render it impossible to construct an entirely satisfactory index of aggregate output of the six industries listed in Table 1. However, a rough approximation to such an index is obtained by using estimates of 'value-added' (sales minus purchases of current supplies from other industries) in the six industries (Table 2). Physical output nearly tripled between 1899 and 1939; almost the entire increase occurred in the first three decades. As population increased 75 percent meanwhile, output per capita of population rose two-thirds.

TABLE 2

Indexes of Output of Six Industries and of Population, 1899-1939

(1899: 100)

	PHYSICAL OUTPUT	POPULATION	OUTPUT PER CAPITA
1899	100	100	100
1909	146	121	120
1919	195	140	139
1929	283	163	174
1939	289	175	165

The indexes of output were computed by the Edgeworth formula, using estimates of 'value-added' as weights (see Fabricant, *Output of Manufacturing*, p. 370), with each date the comparison base for the succeeding date. The estimates of value-added were:

MANUFACTURING: Value-added, as reported by the Census.

AGRICULTURE: Cash income plus value of food consumed on farms minus current expenses. (Net Farm Income and Parity Report, 1943; Bureau of Agricultural Economics, July 1944.) The value-added ratio for 1910 was applied to 1909 and 1899 gross income, extrapolated by data in Strauss and Bean, Gross Farm Income and Indexes of Farm Production (Department of Agriculture, *Technical Bulletin 703*).

MINING: Receipts minus materials, fuel, and power, as reported by the Census; the ratio of value added was interpolated for 1929, when petroleum was excluded from the Census.

STEAM RAILROADS: Operating revenues minus materials and supplies; average of fiscal years before 1919.

ELECTRIC LIGHT AND POWER: Revenue minus fuel, data from Gould, *op. cit.*, Appendix B. The values for the years in the table were interpolated by output. This industry entered the index in 1909.

MANUFACTURED GAS: Revenue minus fuel, data from Gould, *op. cit.*, Appendix B.

NATURAL GAS: Revenue, data from *ibid.*, p. 160.

The output index of Table 2 can be divided into indexes for commodity- and service-producing industries.

INDUSTRIES	1899	1909	1919	1929	1939
Commodity-producing	100	140	180	267	277
Service-producing	100	186	312	400	374

The service industries are too poorly represented to admit of any generalization, but the commodity industries are so fully represented that the index would not be changed much if construction and minor industries now excluded were included. The output of the commodity industries—agriculture, manufacturing, and mining—can be described in virtually the same terms as the aggregate index for the six industries, in which they of course dominate.

The over-all index in Table 2 displays extremely sharp retardation in the 'thirties: the output of the six industries, which had grown at an average rate of 3.5 percent per *year* between 1899 and 1929, now rose only 2.1 percent in a *decade*. In this the index faithfully mirrors its components, for the indexes of the industry groups (manufacturing, agriculture, and mining) , we shall presently see, show little retardation between 1899 and 1929 but sharp retardation thereafter.[2] Two very different explanations have frequently been advanced for the failure of output to grow during the 'thirties. In the one view it is characteristic, indeed inevitable in a maturing private enterprise economy; in the other view it is a sort of economic fault, due to a special combination of political and economic circumstances which may be supplanted by more fundamental and persistent forces that dominated previous history, and which in any case were absent before the Great Depression. A useful discussion of this conflict would take us far beyond the scope of the studies under review, and we must be content to note one fact that bears on the contemporary discussion of the maturity thesis: there is no evidence of long-term retardation before 1929.

Improvements in Quality of Product

We have been discussing indexes of physical output. But output of what? Of the automobiles of 1900, which were sometimes thoughtfully equipped with attachments for harness? Of the gasoline of 1914, which Colorado sought to improve by enacting a statute that set a maximum of 5 percent on solid matter? Clearly we wish an index of output that measures

---

[2] A longer survey might reveal a gradual downward drift in the rate of increase of output since 1870, but the retardation—if it was present at all—was small; see A. F. Burns, *Production Trends in the United States since 1870* (National Bureau of Economic Research, 1934) , pp. 270 ff.

quality as well as quantity, but precisely what do we mean by quality, and how can it be measured?

In everyday discourse we usually understand quality to mean technical characteristics or operating properties. Thus we say the automobile tire of 1937 had eight times the mileage of the tire of 1921, or we say the incandescent lamp produced 3.4 lumens per watt (units of light produced per unit of power consumed) in 1906 and 14.7 in 1937. Occassionally we may tend also to view style changes as improvements but here we tread on dangerous ground: our tastes have altered enough to make the clothes of 1900 amusing to see and embarrassing to wear — as amusing and embarrassing as today's clothes would have appeared to the eyes of 1900.

Some estimate of the magnitude of changes in quality can often be made from changes in the technological properties of a commodity. For example, the tractive power of a steam loco-motive is often used as a measure of its quality. In 1904 the average tractive power of a new locomotive was about 27,000 pounds, and in 1939 about 107,000 pounds.[3] Fabricant's in-dex of output for steam locomotives declined from 366 in 1904 to 29 in 1939—a 92 percent drop. If the production data are corrected for changes in quality, the percentage fall is re-duced to 69 percent.

Such technological measures of quality are subject to def-inite limitations, however. A single measure of quality is usually inappropriate: thus if locomotive quality is meas-ured only by tractive power, other improvements such as fuel economy (the pounds of fuel required to haul 1,000 gross

[3] The 1904 figure is calculated as follows: the distribution by type of loco-motives is estimated from the differences between the number of locomotives of each type reported in 1903 and 1904 in *Statistics of Railways in the United States,* which also gives their tractive power; the tractive power of locomotives installed in 1939 (for which the number of each type is given in *Statistics of Railways, 1939*) is estimated from information in R. P. Johnson, *The Steam Locomotive* (Simmons-Boardman, 1942). The estimate for 1904 is prob-ably low because it is based on average tractive power, not on that of new locomotives.

freight ton-miles fell from 172 in 1920 to 112 in 1940) are ignored; yet we cannot add fuel economy and tractive power. Even if a single technical characteristic were a suitable measure of quality, it would often fail us when new types of product appeared: for example, tractive power is not an appropriate measure of the performance of Diesel and electric locomotives.

There is a second method of measuring changes in quality: to find the ratio of prices of new and old qualities of a product during a period when both are available. This is a direct application of the existing method of combining different goods in an index, except that different qualities are treated —as they should be—as different goods. The method may be illustrated by changes in the quality of gasoline. In 1940 the octane number of 'regular' gasoline rose from 70-72 to 72-74 (as a continuation of the rise from below 65 in 1931, when this system of gasoline rating was adopted by manufacturers). The improved grade sold for 12.9 percent more than the lower grade during the period when both were sold. In measuring the output of gasoline, 100 gallons of the superior grade may be treated as equal to 113 gallons of the inferior grade.

This second method of measuring quality is automatically followed in the construction of the National Bureau indexes of output when the underlying data on outputs are classified finely enough. For instance, by using values as weights, Fabricant counts 1.60 open passenger automobiles as the equivalent of one closed automobile in 1919. But the Census classifications are too broad for any large proportion of quality changes to be measured by this method: thus 1919 and 1939 open passenger automobiles are treated as identical.[4]

How widespread and important have these unmeasured quality improvements been? Fabricant's volume abounds

---

[4]The broadness of the Census classifications is emphasized by the fact that one cannot find in the highly detailed appendices of Fabricant's *Output of Manufacturing Industries* unequivocal evidence of the appearance of a single new manufacturing product between 1899 and 1937.

with descriptions of large technical improvements, and the absence of examples of quality deterioration is also eloquent. Barger lays less emphasis upon quality changes in agriculture and mining, but if systematic account were taken of the increasing rigor of sanitary requirements in milk production, improvements in the qualities of cotton, fruits, meat, etc., and the greater standardization and uniformity of mining products, the improvement of quality in these industries might also be found to be substantial. No enumeration of instances of quality improvement, however, will carry with our statistically-minded age the weight of a specific, over-all number, and quality improvements will continue to be undisputed but easily forgotten until they have been subjected to general measurement.

Household vs. Market

If our indexes of the economy's output have a downward bias because quality improvements are not measured completely, they have an upward bias because they cover a larger proportion of output as production within the household declines. The transfer of activities from household to market has often been mentioned, but it is doubtful that its extent is generally appreciated. A few comparative indexes of this trend suggest large shifts toward prepared foods and greater reliance upon laundries and apartment and hotel housing services (Table 3). There is little doubt (if also little evidence) that restaurant sales have risen substantially relative to total sales of food, and production of clothing in the household has declined.[5] The urban family is also buying in smaller units, and is transferring the storage and parceling of food to retailers.

Nor should only direct transfers of this sort be taken in

[5]Occupational statistics suggest that employees of eating places tripled or quadrupled between 1900 and 1940; population increased only 75 percent. The output of ready-to-wear apparel more than tripled, but factors such as the shift to more fashionable and less durable dress complicate the interpretation.

TABLE 3

Some Measures of the Transfer of Activities
from the Household to the Market

Transfers to Manufacturing	*1899*	*1939*
% of domestically consumed wheat flour used by commercial bakeries	14.8	43.4
Cases of canned vegetables produced per 100 persons	27.5	139.1
Cases of canned fruits produced per 100 persons	4.8	57.3
Transfers to Service Industries	*1900*	*1940*
% of families taking boarders and lodgers	23	5
Employees in commercial laundries and cleaning establishments per 1,000 persons	1.4	3.6
% of families in large cities in multiple-unit dwellings	39.2	57.7

SOURCE: Employees in commercial laundries and cleaning establishments, estimated from Census data; all other data from Stigler, *op. cit.*, pp. 26 ff.

account. The washing machine and the vacuum cleaner, for example, have in effect reduced household work and expanded manufacturing activity.[6] Mechanical fuel systems provide another important example: in 1940, 21.3 percent of the nation's dwelling units were heated by gas or petroleum products, and 64.5 percent used these sources and electricity as cooking fuels.

The greater reliance on the market has been due in part to technological advances such as the invention and improvement of the washing machine. The move to the cities has increased the availability of market provision of processed foods, laundering services, and the like. The average family declined from 4.6 to 3.7 persons in the last 40 years, contributing to a relative growth of multiple-unit dwellings. The increase in the percentage of married women who were in the labor force from 5.6 in 1900 to 16.8 in 1940 was both a cause and an effect of the shift of production to the market. Relative prices have, at least for some commodities, become more favorable to processed goods,[7] and the rise in real in-

[6]The automobile reduced the effort of getting to work—where should one draw the line?

[7]The following data on changes in the relative consumption and prices of bread and flour in cities in four states are pertinent:

come made it possible for more families to buy goods and services (such as prepared baby foods and diaper services) that are time-consuming or unpleasant to perform.

The effects of these transfers upon commercial employment cannot be estimated precisely, but a very rough estimate is that a twentieth of the wage-earners in manufacturing alone were in 1940 providing commodities or services that in 1900 were produced within the household, and of course the shifts to the service industries have been even larger. In many cases the commercial service was no doubt higher in quality, but this transfer is yet another reason why indexes of output should not be confused with indexes of welfare. There may be substantial shifts of activities between household and market within a business cycle, as well as very large shifts during major wars; so even short-run movements of measured output may diverge materially from those of the output of all goods and services.

The Output of Service Industries

As observed above, for only a small segment of service industries—steam railroads and gas and electric utilities—have indexes of output been calculated, whereas they are now available for the preponderant share of commodity-producing industries. This relative neglect of services is attributable in some degree to the absence of pertinent data, but in greater degree to conceptual difficulties, which we now discuss.

If we wished to construct an index of the aggregate output of retailing services, for example, we would have to know first the individual products of the industry: the amounts of stor-

	Ratio: bread to flour consumed (pounds)		Ratio: price of bread to price of flour	
	1901	1935	1901	1935
New York	1.39	4.60	1.76	1.58
Ohio	.57	1.58	1.98	1.65
California	1.06	2.76	2.42	1.69
Louisiana	3.26	6.87	1.34	1.38

Basic data from *Eighteenth Report of the Commissioner of Labor* (1903) and Bureau of Labor Statistics, *Retail Prices*, Bulletin 635 (1937).

age, selling, wrapping, delivery, credit extension, and similar services supplied to consumers. The problems that would be encountered in enumerating these quantities are not different in nature, and perhaps not in magnitude, from those already faced, and solved in varying degree, in the commodity-producing industries. But when one seeks the prices with which to weight these services in constructing a single index, a new problem arises. Rarely is there a separate and definite retail price differential for cash payments vs. a month's credit, delivery of specified frequency, or availability of rarely purchased items. These services are usually supplied jointly in variable amounts. It is as if, in manufacturing, the unit of sales were a variable combination of refrigerators plus toasters plus dishwashers plus washing machines. Indeed, because the 'terms of sale' (credit, promptness of delivery, guarantees, servicing, etc.) are in fact variable components of the output of commodity-producing industries, the same problem is present in measuring their output. But perhaps because it is believed that these 'terms of sale' are relatively unimportant—which is not intuitively obvious—the recorded price is attributed entirely to the physical product.

The types of data that must be enumerated are admittedly a serious obstacle to calculating indexes of service outputs.[8] Is the additional obstacle of the absence of an explicit price system insurmountable? I think not. There exists an implicit price system for the components of retailing service, to continue our example, and it could be uncovered by statistical analysis of appropriate data. By classifying retail stores of a given type with respect to these various services, we would be able to isolate the effect of a particular service on the retail margin. Fragments of information on this subject are already available. But to construct indexes of service outputs will be a very large task.[9]

[8]Indeed in certain industries such as domestic service this obstacle seems decisive.

[9]As a first approximation, we may measure (e.g.) retailing output by

A different type of price problem is confronted in public enterprise — governments and nonprofit institutions. The 'buyer's' common inability to determine freely the quantities he wishes to purchase of the products and services of such groups means that we cannot attribute proportionality of prices to marginal significances—the fundamental basis for combining heterogeneous economic quantities. It must suffice here to observe that this problem has received much careful attention from students of national income, and apparently has not yet been solved to their satisfaction.

In still other service categories even the specific content of output is debatable. We may cite as very different examples soldiers and teachers. In such fields it is not now possible even to enumerate the specific services that are sought. Perforce we adopt the convention that output is identical with input, or leave output unmeasured.

Composition of Output

Perhaps the first discovery of a person who begins to investigate the composition of output is the existence of a vexing problem of classification. We expect the broadest classifications—manufactures vs. agricultural products, consumer vs. producer goods, and the like—to be difficult to define: the enormously diverse details of economic life offer innumerable challenges to classifications and invitations to arbitrary decisions. But the difficulties persist even in narrower classifications. There is no natural unit of analysis, unless it is the individual transaction, corresponding to the man in population studies or the isotope in chemistry: almost every 'product' can be subclassified by quality, location and time of production, use, etc.

Other difficulties are raised by the different interests of the

---

physical volume of goods sold, each type of goods being weighted by the retail margin per unit. This procedure is analogous to that used in measuring physical output of commodity-producing industries when quality changes are not taken into account.

data collector and the data user. The collector must report the complex details of economic life in few enough classes to be comprehended, and with due regard to comparability between classes and between times. The data user, on the other hand, commonly has much more specialized interests, and these interests are often dictated by problems that do not spring into prominence until a generation or more after the data have been reported.

The effects of the absence of a 'natural unit' in output studies and the reporting methods of data collectors may be illustrated with respect to stability of composition. We might wish to compare the relative stability of the composition of outputs of food and machinery in manufacturing (using, say, the coefficient of correlation between values-added by individual products within the two classes at two dates). The result, which would be that the composition of machinery output was much more stable than that of food, would be completely pre-determined by the classifications: almost all machinery is grouped into three or four classes so composition cannot vary much.

Certain significant aspects of composition, however, can be investigated with tolerable accuracy. Three are considered here: the relative growths of consumer durable and nondurable goods; the trends of output in the six major industry categories; and the interrelations between changes in outputs of broad categories and of more specific products of which they are composed.

The Flow of Consumer Goods

It is not easy to form a general impression of the growth in the output of consumer goods from the numerous indexes of outputs of specific goods in the several National Bureau studies. To reduce the complexity of the picture, several indexes were combined (see Table 4). These indexes do not, of course, parallel exactly the corresponding consumption series. The former take no account of exports or imports or

TABLE 4

Output Indexes of Consumer Goods, 1899-1939

	1899	1909	1919	1929	1939
Productivity Studies					
Food	100	144	196	290	324
Beverages	100	147	53	......	251
Tobacco products	100	143	230	333	400
Textiles	100	158	176	263	313
Shoes	100	127	150	165	186
Automobile, tires, and gasoline	......	100	769	2,430	2,051
Six industries	100	146	195	283	289
W. H. Shaw's Study					
Consumer perishables	100	141	170	239	295
Consumer semi-durables	100	145	188	334	272
Consumer durables	100	148	318	622	551
All consumer goods	100	143	191	306	320
Population	100	121	140	163	175

SOURCES: Food consists of manufactured food plus potatoes, poultry and eggs, dairy products (weighted only by value of fluid milk), fruits, and noncommercial truck products. Barger's and Fabricant's indexes were combined by value of product, estimated from *Agricultural Statistics* and the *Census of Manufactures.*

Shoes are leather and rubber, combined by Census data on value.

Automobiles, tires and tubes (included after 1919), and petroleum refining were combined by Census data on value.

There is some duplication, as when fruits are included in both agriculture and manufactured products, some inclusion of producer goods (rugs for offices), and some omissions (food grown off farms). The indexes are therefore only rough measures.

Shaw's series are from Finished Commodities since 1879, *Occasional Paper 3* (National Bureau of Economic Research, 1941).

of inventory changes, and the outputs of durable goods in any year may bear little relation to the use of such goods during the year. More comprehensive indexes compiled by William H. Shaw, which do allow for exports and imports and make a finer allocation between producer and consumer goods, are also given.[10]

[10]See Finished Commodities since 1879, *Occasional Paper 3* (National Bureau of Economic Research, 1941). Shaw estimates (from independent evidence), the proportions of a commodity (e.g., coal) that are used by producers and consumers, whereas we do this only roughly by the system of weights. He eliminates price changes by the use of price indexes for 44 groups of commodities, whereas prices of individual commodities are used for this purpose in the productivity studies.

The output of food rose rapidly—to three times its 1899 level. Per capita consumption of food, measured by weight or calories, was probably more or less stable (indeed, falling gradually) during this period when per capita food output rose three-quarters. The rise in output reflects both the shift to more expensive foods (vegetables, dairy products, citrus fruits) and the further processing of food (flour into bread, the canning of vegetables) before it leaves manufacturing. The lesser importance of food grown and consumed on farms also raises the index. The increase in the output of food would be even larger if we could take account of the greater proportion purchased in restaurants.

Of the four groups of nondurable goods in Table 4, all except one (alcoholic beverages) rose more than the aggregate output of the three commodity-producing industries covered by the productivity studies. Shaw's index of the output of nondurable consumer goods rose almost 200 percent from 1899 to 1939, and conforms fairly well with this finding of rapid growth. But his index of the total output of all goods rose considerably more than that of our three commodity-producing industries,[11] and yields the opposite conclusion, namely, that consumer perishables and semi-durables rose less rapidly than total output. Each approach has its shortcomings, so it is probably unsafe to conclude more than that the increases in nondurables and in total output were of the same order of magnitude. If the increases in productivity (relative to population) of commodity-producing industries lead to a relative decline in the share of consumer nondurables, as some believe, the tendency is relatively weak. But Shaw's indexes clearly demonstrate that consumer durables have increased more rapidly than nondurables (or than producer goods).

[11]The two series are:

	1899	1909	1919	1929	1939
Three Commodity-Producing Industries	100	140	180	267	277
Shaw's Total Output	100	144	206	323	331

Output of Six Industries

The relative contributions of the six industries to the total 'value-added' of the group are presented in Table 5. The most striking results, which would survive in more accurate measures, are the rapid decline of agriculture after 1919, the approximately offsetting increases in manufacturing, and

TABLE 5

Composition of Output, Measured by Percentage of Value-Added, by Each of Six Industries, 1899-1939

	1899	1909	1919	1929	1939
Agriculture	30.8	31.5	29.8	18.8	15.9
Manufacturing	48.9	47.1	52.5	59.4	61.7
Mining	5.6	5.3	5.3	5.5	6.4
Electric light and power	......	1.0	1.4	3.6	4.9
Gas	.8	1.1	.7	1.3	1.8
Steam railroads	13.8	14.0	10.3	11.4	9.3
Total	99.9	100.0	100.0	100.0	100.0

the similar offset of the growth of electric light and power by the decline of steam railroads (Chart 1).[12]

The decade increases, summarized in Table 6, are somewhat misleading because of the effects of business cycles: 1899 was a peak year, 1909 a year of expansion, 1919 a year of both contraction and recovery, 1929 a peak year, and 1939 a year of expansion. Consequently, the increase from 1929 to 1939 is low relative to the underlying trend, and that from 1919 to 1929 high. From Chart 1, however, it appears that the secular rate of increase in manufacturing was virtually constant to 1929, and the rate of increase of output in agriculture and mining fell only slowly. The rates of growth in the other, less diversified, industries fell more rapidly.

The movements of output in the six industries are materially influenced by their definitions. We need not con-

[12]The annual data are given in the Appendix. The vertical scale in Chart 1 (and subsequent charts) measures only percentage changes in output; the reader may find it convenient to transcribe the scale to a separate strip of paper.

CHART 1

Indexes of Output in Six Industries
1899 – 1940

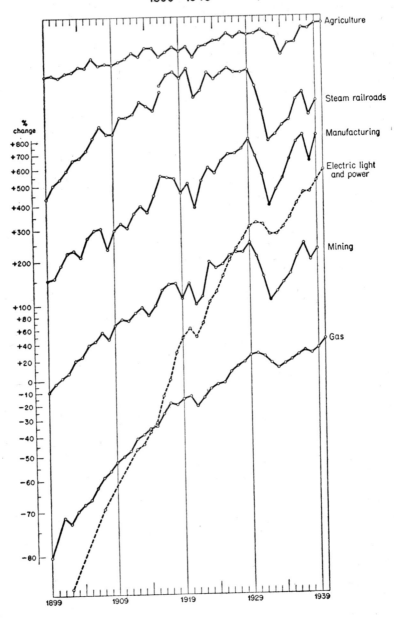

TABLE 6

Percentage Changes in the Outputs of Six Industries and in their Aggregate Output, by Decades, 1899-1939

	1899-1909	1909-1919	1919-1929	1929-1939
Agriculture	11.1	12.6	15.2	10.4
Manufacturing	57.8	40.6	63.9	2.7
Mining	84.0	27.3	66.1	−5.9
Electric light and power	......	339.0	133.3	67.7
Gas	138.6	78.2	48.8	15.3
Steam railroads	80.6	66.1	7.5	−25.0
Aggregate output	45.8	35.5	45.4	1.9

Index for electric light and power for 1909 estimated by linear interpolation.

cern ourselves with the propriety of the definitions at any given time. When a reasonably clear distinction between manufacturing and mining or between trade and services is sought, the conventional nature of these categories soon becomes apparent. It is more relevant to observe the effects of even minor changes in classification. For example, in 1909, 124,000 persons in power laundries were reported in manufacturing; in 1939, 254,000 persons in the same industry were reported in services. Again, in 1914, 17,700 persons were in automobile repair shops—in manufacturing; in 1939 the number was 134,000—in services. If the Census Bureau had retained these industries in manufacturing, its personnel would be about 2 percent higher in 1909, and about 5 percent higher in 1939. These variations in practice were easy to cope with, but have there been important shifts of activities between industries that are not so directly reported?

The distribution of productive activities among broad industry groups usually shifts slowly, but under the impact of changes in technology and mores the aggregate shift is sometimes large in even relatively short periods. When we are discussing the importance of a cultural-economic group such as farmers, the shift of activities to the factory requires no special treatment—the decline of agriculture is no less real whether due to a shift away of activities or the release of workers on farms due to technological progress. But if we are interested in the proportion of resources necessary to provide food at a given level of preparation, a shift of activities leads us to misjudge changes in the relative share of resources necessary to satisfy our needs. To document the importance of such shifts, we examine in some detail the case of agriculture.

The movement of food processing away from the farm is as ancient as the growth of cities. The transfer had gone far in cheese and the slaughter of animals by 1900, as Table 7 indicates. Other industry boundaries were also shifting: the complementary percentages understate the relative growth of factory output because the processing of livestock by retailers also declined. The indexes of agricultural and manufacturing output and employment during our period would not be affected significantly by recognizing this shift.[13]

TABLE 7

Shift of Food Processing from the Farm, 1879-1939

Percentage of Production on Farms[a]

	1879	1899	1939
Cheese	11.2	5.5	
Butter	96.4	71.8	21.3
Percentage of Slaughter on Farms[b]			
Cattle		8.3	4.3
Calves		17.5	8.5
Hogs		26.7	20.7
Sheep and lambs		4.2	3.1

[a]E. E. Vial, *Producion and Consumption of Manufactured Dairy Products,* Department of Agriculture, *Technical Bulletin 722* (1940); 1939 data from *Agricultural Statistics.*
[b]Barger and Landsberg, *op. cit.,* p. 9n.

A much more important shift is involved in the replacement of horses and mules by tractors and automobiles. In 1900 there were no automobiles on farms and virtually no tractors; in fact, both became prominent only during World War I. In 1940 there were 4,100,000 automobiles, 1,000,-000 trucks, and 1,600,000 tractors on American farms. E. G.

[13]The labor requirements for these food-processing activities on the farm are not known. The food-processing industries required about 20,000 man-years in 1939 to handle the increase in the proportion of output that was done in factories compared with the proportion in 1899.

McKibben and R. A. Griffin estimated the saving in farm labor due to this shift, on the following assumptions:[14]

1) The tractor increased the output of a worker in field operations 50 percent, and is used 300 hours a year.
2) About 7 million horses and mules have been displaced, with annual savings of:
    a) 50 hours of labor caring for each animal;
    b) 35 hours of labor caring for each of 1,750,000 young horses required to replace the 7 million;
    c) 17.6 man-hours per acre in raising feed, with 3.5 crop acres and 1.8 pasture acres required per horse and half as much per colt.

The change to mechanical power thus reduced direct labor requirements about 1,200 million man-hours. The labor saved by the introduction of the automobile and truck was not estimated; if it is arbitrarily set at 100 hours per vehicle, another 500 million man-hours of agricultural labor was saved.

It is difficult to convert agricultural man-hours into man-years; much of the saving was no doubt reflected in shorter working hours and less help from the farm family. Yet it seems conservative to estimate that the farm labor force would have been 5 or 10 percent larger in 1940 had these shifts—which came within twenty years—not occurred.

The Whole and the Parts

Subject to the pervasive limitations of information, one can subdivide the indexes of output almost endlessly. For example, we can follow Fabricant in classifying manufacturing industries under 17 major headings; then food, for example, can be subdivided into 25 subclasses such as flour; and this in turn into 7 products of flour mills. Nor need we stop here: wheat flour—one of the 7 products—can obviously be subdivided further.

[14]*Tractors, Trucks, and Automobiles* (National Research Project, Report A-9, 1938). Their results have been brought up to 1939.

As the products become more specific, we encounter greater variety of trend and amplitude of fluctuation, as we should expect. Shifts between kinds of flour will have little impact on all flour, and shifts between breadstuffs and vegetables will partly cancel, leaving the output of food relatively unaffected. The tendency toward stability as the industry coverage is extended is illustrated in Charts 2, 3, and 4, which portray trends of four kinds of flour, of the food industries that ranked among the first four in 1899 or 1939, and of the broad industry categories that ranked among the first four at either date.[15]

We are not surprised to find evidence of retardation in the outputs of virtually all established industries making a relatively narrow range of products. In *Production Trends in the United States since 1870* Arthur F. Burns amply demonstrated this retardation to be a characteristic of a progressive economy.[16] One may roughly generalize that we do not wish to have the old products if we can have the new ones. Nor is this ubiquitous decline in the rate of growth of outputs of individual products or industries incompatible with relative stability in the rate of growth of aggregate output, as the negligible retardation of output in manufacturing, mining, and agriculture before 1929 testifies.

It is a natural step to test the hypothesis: can we say that the greater the heterogeneity of the rates of growth in specific industries, the greater is the rate of growth of the industry group comprising them? There is strong evidence to suggest that the answer is 'yes'.

A first test of the hypothesis can be made by comparing the rates of growth (from 1899 to 1929) of the outputs of 36

15Each of the rankings was confined to industries for which indexes of output were available.

16Ch. IV. Burns relied chiefly on annual series, and although his indexes do not include as many products as the productivity studies, the period covered was longer and cyclical influences on estimates of trends could be minimized.

CHART 2

Indexes of Output of Leading Flour Mill Products
1899 – 1939

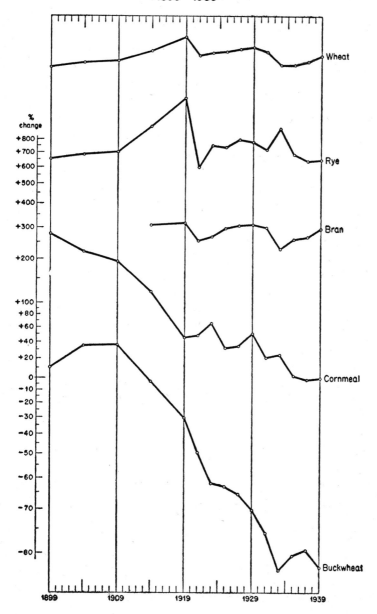

CHART 3

Indexes of Output of Leading Food Industries
1899 – 1939

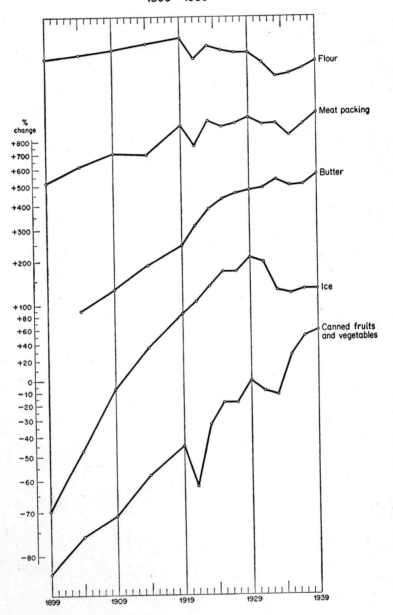

CHART 4

Indexes of Output of Five Industry Groups and All Manufacturing
1899 – 1939

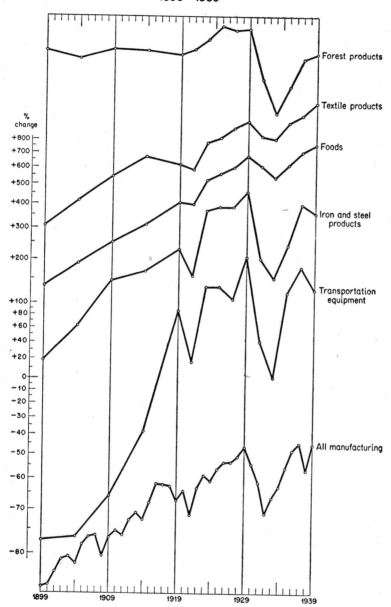

%
change

+800
+700
+600
+500
+400
+300
+200
+100
+80
+60
+40
+20
0
−10
−20
−30
−40
−50
−60
−70
−80

Forest products

Textile products

Foods

Iron and steel
products

Transportation
equipment

All manufacturing

1899   1909   1919   1929   1939

agricultural products with the rates of growth of 28 food products in manufacturing.[17] The comparison is congruent

	AGRICULTURE	MANUFACTURING
Percentage increase in aggregate output	44	233
Number of products	36	28
Percentage increase in outputs of individual products:		
First Quartile	17	54
Second Quartile	79	154
Third Quartile	215	608
Inter-Quartile ratio $\dfrac{Q_3 - Q_1}{Q_2}$	2.51	3.60

with the hypothesis: both variability and the average rate of increase were larger in manufacturing than in agriculture.

Burns' study of production trends for a longer period also revealed greater variability in the growth of outputs in the more rapidly growing industry sectors. Moreover, the same correspondence of growth and variability occurred through time: the trends of the outputs of individual products showed greater divergences in periods when average growth was more rapid.[18]

Rapidity of the growth of total output is, it seems, associated with wide dispersion of trends in individual industries. This suggests a concrete sense in which one may speak of the clash between security and progress: the rapid growth of aggregate output implies the even more rapid growth of new and the decline of old industries. It was as inevitable that the rapid growth of the radio industry should virtually destroy the player piano industry (the output of which fell from 144,000 in 1925 to 1,690 in 1931) as that the rapid growth of the automobile industry should virtually destroy the carriage industry (the output of which fell from over 900,000 in 1899 to 3,600 in 1929). We should like to have both a rapid increase in aggregate output and stability in

[17]The agricultural products are those for which Barger gives outputs since 1899. In manufacturing the criteria for inclusion were: (a) data back to 1899, (b) a value of product of at least $5 million in 1899 or $20 million in 1929.

[18]*Op. cit.*, pp. 61-2, and 243.

its composition—the former to keep pace with expanding wants, and the latter to avoid the losses of specialized equipment of entrepreneurs and crafts of employees and creating 'sick' industries in which resources are less mobile than customers. It is highly probable that the goals are inconsistent.

CHAPTER 2

Trends in Employment

Labor is the only input for which we have relatively detailed data in the industries covered by indexes of output. Labor employment, however, is of decisive importance in economic policy, and it is easy to document also labor's great, indeed preponderant, quantitative role in the operation of the economic system. In 1919, midway through our period, in the six industries employee compensation plus entrepreneurial net income (almost all of which was in agriculture) amounted to 87 percent of the income originating in these industries; in the economy as a whole these labor returns were 76 percent of national income.

The employment of labor in industry is part of a broader economic problem. The time and energy a person has to spend on a multitude of desirable activities is limited, and he seeks to allocate these scarce resources efficiently among the competing ends. For purposes of social welfare, the economy's labor resources are its adult population. Conventional measures of the labor force therefore suffer from the same ambiguity as measures of output, which exclude productive activity within the household. Although it is not a matter of indifference whether men shave themselves or hire barbers, the crossing of the boundary between household and market leads to a much larger difference in commercial labor force and commercial output than it does in the welfare of the community. As we have observed, the index of output tends to rise too rapidly because it omits the declining share of household production; and similarly the index of the labor force rises too rapidly because it does not include the declining share of household laborers. Moreover, the increased leisure accruing to persons outside the labor force is not taken into account in indexes of output (or input), although the increased leisure accruing to those in the labor force may be estimated roughly.

If we confine ourselves to the commercial labor force, the number of laborers may be measured by the number of persons employed or by the number both working and seeking work—in census terminology, the gainfully occupied. This category is not without its difficulties: does it include, in addition to the employed, those actively seeking work and those who would accept suitable jobs? To be in the labor force, must a person be seeking a job for which he is qualified, and if so, who is to determine his qualifications? Is the number seeking work strongly influenced—and if so, in what direction—by the level of wages? Fortunately or unfortunately, our answers to these and similar questions are irrelevant to the past; the unique number reported in the decennial census is the sum of millions of individuals' interpretations of questions such as,

Are you seeking work? [To be answered in the affirmative if registered at an employment agency, or a new worker in a mining town where there is unemployment, or if work was not sought because of illness, etc.]

Are you a professional football player, without another occupation [and hence outside the labor force]?

and the intriguing query, Do you choose not to work?

Let us hope, and assume, that our difficulties are unimportant or that they have been solved by a public continuously called upon to face hard issues. We may then form a notion of the relative importance of our six industries in the labor force (Table 8). Each industry except agriculture had about the same share of the labor force in 1940 as in 1900 (although the combination of transportation and public utilities conceals a sizable shift from the former to the latter). But as agriculture's share of the labor force was halved during these four decades, the fraction of the labor force in the six industries fell from two-thirds in 1900 to a half in 1940.

TABLE 8

Percentage Distribution of the Gainfully Occupied
by Industries, 1900-1940

	1900	1910	1920	1930	1940
Industries Covered by Indexes of Output					
Agriculture	37.9	31.6	27.4	22.1	18.0
Manufacturing	21.6	22.5	26.1	23.0	23.9
Mining	2.6	2.9	3.0	2.5	2.2
Transportation & public utilities	5.0	6.8	7.4	7.0	5.0
Total	67.1	63.8	63.9	54.6	49.1
Industries Not Covered					
Construction	5.6	6.3	5.3	6.4	6.9
Trade	8.9	9.6	9.9	12.7	14.4
Finance	1.0	1.4	1.9	3.0	3.1
Government	2.7	3.6	4.5	5.0	6.1
Private services	12.2	13.0	11.7	15.1	17.3
Other	2.4	2.2	2.8	3.2	3.0
Total	32.8	36.1	36.1	45.4	50.8
Population (millions)	76.1	92.4	106.5	123.1	132.0
Gainfully occupied (millions)	29.1	37.4	42.4	48.8	53.3

SOURCE: Based upon Daniel Carson's *Industrial Composition of Manpower in the United States, 1870-1940* (unpublished). The scope of the industries differs in minor respects from that in the production studies: manufacturing includes hand trades; transportation and public utilities is also broader than gas, electricity, and railroads. The persons whose industry was not reported (6.3 percent of all persons in 1940 but much less in earlier years) are distributed among the industries in proportion to reported numbers; this procedure overstates the relative number in agriculture.

Employment in Six Industries

The allocation of unemployed persons among industries is hazardous, and in an economy where labor is mobile it is also misleading. In any event, the number of persons actually employed is more relevant to the query, how much labor has been required to produce the outputs of the six industries? Before we turn to the answer, however, some gaps in the data on employment must be summarized.

In agriculture we do not have knowledge of employment proper and perforce substitute the number in the labor force (defined as farmers and adult male laborers on farms). In manufacturing continuous data are available only for wage earners (see Chart 5 and the Appendix), but tolerably accurate estimates can be made of all employees and proprietors (Table 9). In mining there are huge gaps in the record; we have a total for employees only since 1929. The series on mining in Chart 5 is based upon man-hours of employment in the mining industries covered by output indexes (and omits 1903-28), while that in Table 9 includes only employees in coal mining.[1] The number of employees on steam railroads, in electric light and power, and gas (excluding natural gas before 1929) are reasonably complete and continuous. The omission of employees in mining other than coal miners from the aggregate in Table 9 imparts a small downward bias.

TABLE 9

Employment in Six Industries, 1899-1939

	1899	1909	1919	1929	1939	NUMBER IN 1939 (1,000)
		INDEX OF EMPLOYMENT (1929: 100)				
Agriculture[a]	91	102	103	100	87	7,445
Manufacturing	51	73	100	100	92	9,178
Coal Mining	63	110	119	100	82	538[b]
Electric light and power		21	41	100	93	271
Gas	33	60	80	100	95	133
Steam railroads	55	89	116	100	60	1,007
Index for Six Industries	67	86	103	100	87	
Number (1,000)	14,264	18,365	21,874	21,338	18,570	

[a]Data are for 1900, 1910, etc. The series refers to farmers and adult male laborers; that of all gainfully occupied is:

1900	1910	1920	1930	1940
104	111	109	100	88

[b]Employees and proprietors in all mining numbered 887 thousand in 1939.

Employment grew much more slowly than output in each of the six industries. Indeed employment in agriculture, manufacturing, coal mining (and probably all mining), and steam railroads had stopped growing by the 'twenties, and the gas and electric industries reached this stage by 1930. Aggregate employment in the six industries, which rose a third from 1899 to 1919, fell slightly in the 'twenties, and by 1939 had fallen almost a sixth from the 1919 peak in our decennial data. During the forty years employment in the

[1]Wage-earners in coal mining were 64 percent of all wage-earners in mining in both 1929 and 1939, and doubtless a considerably higher percentage before 1929. In 1939 they were 61 percent of wage-earners, salaried employees, and proprietors in mining.

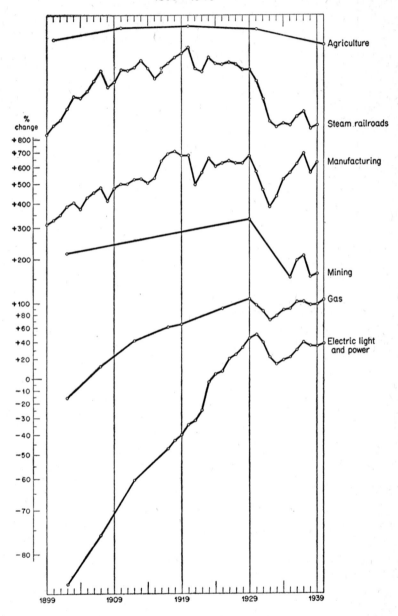

CHART 5

Indexes of Employment in Six Industries
1899 – 1940

%
change

+800
+700
+600
+500
+400
+300
+200
+100
+80
+60
+40
+20
0
−10
−20
−30
−40
−50
−60
−70
−80

Agriculture

Steam railroads

Manufacturing

Mining

Gas

Electric light
and power

1899   1909   1919   1929   1939

six industries increased 28 percent while the aggregate labor force increased 83 percent (Tables 8 and 9).

The increase in the number employed in the various industries substantially overstates the increase in the input of labor time because hours of work were sharply reduced.

	AVERAGE HOURS WORKED	
	1900	1940
Manufacturing (per week)	60	40
Mining (per shift)	9.1	7.3
Manufactured gas (per week)	52 (1914)	41
Electric light and power (per week)	46 (1917)	40
Steam railroads (per week)	60.6 (1916)	46.6

SOURCES

Manufacturing: Fabricant, *Employment in Manufacturing*, p. 14.
Mining: Barger and Schurr, *op. cit.*, p. 72.
Manufactured gas and electric light and power: Gould, *op. cit.*, pp. 70-1, 120.
Steam railroads: *Statistics of Railways of the United States, 1920*, p. xix; 1940, p. 62.

The decrease in hours of work in agriculture was much less (perhaps 5 percent) than in the five groups in the tabulation, but even including this large group the average hours of work per week in all six industries fell about a fifth during the four decades. As this decrease nearly offsets the increase in the number employed, man-hours of employment in these industries were about equal in 1939 and 1899.

Employment in the Service Industries

Since aggregate employment in the six industries reached its peak about 1920, the growing labor force must have been absorbed by the private service industries and government. These fields have not been explored sufficiently to be described in detail, but a summary of employment trends in selected service industries may be of interest.

The position of the private service industries in economic statistics is anomalous, for our knowledge of them is almost unbelievably small. We know from Census reports, the chief and often sole source in such fields, the employment in making and the output of fire extinguishers for 16 years from 1899 to 1939, when a peak of one thousand persons was reached. We have very approximate figures for five years during this period on 'gainfully occupied' private family servants, who numbered more than two million in 1940.

It is easy to explain why the Census has provided more detail on a few factory employees than on two thousand times as many domestic servants. The smallness of the employing unit, the difficulty of defining output, the greater social concern with employment and output in manufacturing, the ubiquity of the service industries, and the absence of a dramatized industrial revolution—these and other factors readily explain, even if they do not justify, the difference in our empirical knowledge.

The same emphasis has ruled in economic analysis. Our general textbooks have dozens of references to manufacturing or utilities for one to the service industries; economics seems to be visualized as the study of hordes of men and women pouring into and out of 40-acre buildings. By implication, when not by explicit statement, manufacturing is the center of gravity of the economic system. Theories of monopoly probably owe their current popularity in considerable degree to this viewpoint.

Yet the public and private services (government, trade, finance, and service in Table 8) contained a quarter of the labor force in 1900 and about 40 percent in 1940. This sector of the economy is coming to be better appreciated and there is promise that it will receive more attention from economists. The service industries as a whole cannot be discussed here, but we briefly describe employment or labor force trends in three large service industries for which studies have been or are being made.

The service industries, for which estimates of employment or the labor force are given (Table 10), employed about half of the persons in the 'services' category in 1940, and were the only industries, besides eating and drinking places, to employ more than a million people. Only in the services is a million employees feasible as a criterion of bigness.

TABLE 10

Persons in Domestic Service, Education and Trade, 1900-1940

	DOMESTIC SERVANTS[a]	TOTAL NUMBER	THOUSANDS EDUCATION[b]		Wholesale and Retail Trade[c]	
			ELEMENTARY AND SECONDARY	HIGHER	*Census of Occupations*	*Census of Distribution*
1900	1,509	509	480	29	2,161	
1910	1,867	639	594	45	3,389	
1920	1,485	835	773	62	4,115	
1929						6,808
1930	2,025	1,085	985	105	5,828	
1935						5,930
1939						6,898
1940	2,098	1,162	1,015	147	6,756	
			INDEX (1900: 100)			
1900	100	100	100	100	100	
1910	124	126	124	155	157	
1920	98	164	161	214	190	
1930	134	213	205	362	270	
1940	139	228	211	507	313	

Data for domestic servants from Stigler, *op. cit.*, p. 4; those for education are from the Biennial Survey of Education; and those for trade are estimates based on the *Census of Occupations* and the *Census of Distribution*.

[a]This series is too low but it is comparable through time; it refers to persons attached to the industry, whether employed or unemployed.

[b]Academic personnel only; the number is for teaching positions in elementary and secondary schools in recent years, and a mixture of positions and employees in earlier years; the number in higher education is for employees.

[c]The totals include proprietors and, in the *Census of Distribution*, the average number of employees during the year.

The extreme paucity of our knowledge about these large fields of employment is well illustrated by the discordant series for trade. According to the censuses of retailing and wholesaling, the number in trade was stable between 1929 and 1939; according to the *Census of Occupations*, it rose almost a million.[2] Was one of the largest American industries stable or growing fairly rapidly?

The diversity of the growth of employment in these in-

[2]The two series are comparable in coverage, and the discrepancy is not diminished by allowing for unemployment, difference in dates, part-time workers, etc. It is possible to give reasons for distrusting both sources. The *Census of Distribution* has one defect the importance of which is not commonly recognized: as it is taken at the end of the year, after a fair fraction of retailers operating during the year have closed shop, employees of these stores are not included in the year's average. The undercount may easily be 5 percent, varying with the stage of the business cycle.

dustries is perhaps an unnecessary reminder of the heterogeneity within the service group. Domestic service had
reached a plateau at the outbreak of the war; education grew
at a high and increasing rate until 1930, but thereafter its
rate of growth was less than that of the labor force; and trade
(necessarily measured by the *Census of Occupations*) grew
more than twice as rapidly as the labor force until 1930 and
continued to grow in relative importance, though at a decreasing rate, until 1940.

The Measurement of Employment

Figures on employment are simply sums of numbers of men
or man-hours; they disregard changes in the quality of
the labor force. No one can doubt their utility for many
problems, the chief of which are concerned with unemployment. But such figures do not accurately measure the draft
on the productive resources of the nation: for this purpose
it is as wrong to add different types of laborers as it is to add
(without weighting) wood and mechanical pencils in making
an index of output—as wrong in principle and often as wrong
quantitatively.

No definite conclusion can be drawn about changes in
the average quality of the entire labor force. Some factors
have been working in the direction of improved quality:

1) A smaller percentage of the labor force now consists
of very young workers (Table 11).

TABLE 11

Percentage of the Labor Force Consisting of Young People
1900, 1930, and 1940

AGE	1900	1930	1940
		AGRICULTURE	
10-13	6.0	2.0	
14-15	4.4	2.5	1.7
16-19	11.5*	10.5	9.2
		NONAGRICULTURE	
10-13	1.0	.1	
14-15	2.7	.4	.2
16-19	10.0*	7.6	5.2

Based on Census reports on occupations: the 1940 data are not wholly
comparable because of the change from 'gainfully occupied' to 'labor force'.
*Estimated.

2) The reduction in working hours (by perhaps a fifth on the average), the mechanization of the heaviest kinds of work, and the decreased incidence and improved treatment of industrial diseases must have tended to increase the productivity of labor. So many chapters in the chronicle of health and vigor of the labor force remain to be written, however, that no generalization can safely be drawn.

3) Educational training has substantially increased. In 1900 there was only one technician (engineer, chemist, etc.) for every 400 workers; in 1940, there was one for every 130. Alba Edwards estimates that semi-skilled workers rose from 14.7 to 21.0 percent of the labor force between 1910 and 1940, and unskilled workers fell from 36 to 25.9.[3] The great increase in the formal schooling of the population is generally believed to have increased labor productivity.

In addition, there are such intangible and unexplored factors as discipline, morale, and enterprise. A fascinating and important story begs to be written on the quality of the labor force.

Changes in the quality of the entire labor force must necessarily be very gradual under normal conditions. In individual trades the situation is quite different. The glass-blowers are the textbook example: in the late nineteenth century this craft was among the aristocracy of the labor force in terms of skill or earnings, but mechanization largely replaced them with ordinary semi-skilled laborers. A proper index of labor input in the glass container industry would discount the nominal increase in employment. The recognition of changes in labor quality in particular industries may often change radically the picture of trends in the quantities of labor employed in production.

[3]*Comparative Occupation Statistics for the United States, 1870 to 1940* (Washington, D. C. 1943), p. 187.

CHAPTER 3

Trends in Output per Worker

The output of the economy may be viewed as the product of employment of workers and output per worker. We have discussed changes in employment in the preceding chapter; let us now turn to changes in output per worker.

Output per worker is determined by two factors: first, the productivity of labor; second, the quantity and quality of the other resources cooperating with labor. Output per worker rises when the workers are more skilled and work with greater intensity, and it rises also when they are given better equipment, more efficient plant-layouts, and better materials.

We may, as a rule, view an increase in output per worker as evidence of economic progress whether it stems from improvements in labor or improvements in the cooperating resources. A general increase in output due to improvements in the productivity of labor is an unmixed blessing if it comes from better training, better minds, and better physiques: we are in effect adding to the hands that run our economic system without—as the classical economists sometimes believed necessary—adding to the mouths that consume its product. Similarly, increases in output per worker achieved by increasing the quantity or improving the quality of cooperating resources imply that we have extended our mastery over nature or over ignorance: we can live better without working harder.

The index is not infallible, of course. To the extent, for example, that increases in output per worker are obtained by persuading the workers to strike a pace that depletes their reserves—as was at times the case during the war—the increases are promises of economic retrogression rather than signs of economic progress. Or again, if we increase capital per worker by the expedient of utilizing less of the labor force, we may be moving backward instead of forward. These and other qualifications are of some importance, and will be discussed below, but they are not likely to upset the interpretation of long-run increases in output per worker as a sign, indeed a rough measure, of economic progress.

We must remember that a recorded increase in output per worker may be due to either labor or the cooperating resources. The temptation to attribute an increase to only one source—usually labor, in part because it is more easily measured—is strong but must be resisted. The attribution of all changes in total output to one of the inputs is an error. And the error may lead to economic waste, for if all changes in output are attributed to one input, there may be no inducement to increase the quantity or improve the quality of the cooperating resources.

Changes in Output per Worker

By dividing the rough index of aggregate output (Table 2) by that of aggregate employment (Table 9), we derive a series for output per worker rising from 100 in 1899 to 222 in 1939. That is, output per worker in the six industries rose on

1899	1909	1919	1929	1939
100	113	127	189	222

the average 122 percent, an average of 14 percent each decade except in the 'twenties, when the increase was almost 50 percent. If labor were measured in man-hours instead of workers, the increase in output per unit of labor would be about 200 percent.[1] The shift to man-hours would also reduce the bulge in the rate of increase in the 'twenties, because hours of labor fell less in this decade than in the other three decades.[2]

Labor requirements per unit of output declined markedly and persistently (Chart 6). The smallest reduction, in agri-

[1]Fabricant, Occasional Paper 23.
[2]In manufacturing the average hours of work per week fell 4, 9, 3, and 18 percent respectively in the four decades.

CHART 6

Indexes of Employment per Unit of Output in Six Industries
1899 – 1940

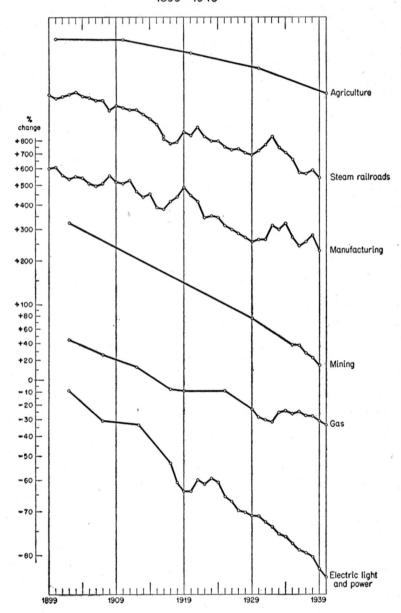

culture, was 40 percent.[3] Of the six industries, gas alone
experienced a pronounced decline in the rate of decrease
in labor requirements.

In other words, if the 1940 products of these industries
could have been produced with the techniques of 1900, they
would have required the entire labor force, working more
hours than were customary in 1940. Instead, these outputs
were produced by less than half of the 1940 labor force.

This is a somewhat dramatic method of summarizing
the enormous gains that accumulate almost surreptitiously
through technical advance. But the gains need to be dramatized. The losses resulting from widespread unemployment of resources are much more obvious. They are serious
and no one will deny the urgency of finding ways to min-
imize them. There is, however, a dangerous tendency to talk
as if the avoidance of unemployment were the only problem
of social policy—unemployment must be avoided 'at all costs'.
Unfortunately, it is difficult to harmonize the objectives of
full employment and rapid economic progress. This is not
to argue that unemployment should be accepted fatalistically
as the price of progress, but it does argue strongly for giving
due consideration to progress in devising measures to combat
unemployment. The fundamental economic problem is not
merely to maximize employment—this goal might possibly
be attained by freezing the economy at a moment of full employment—but also to achieve a large and growing output.

Output per Worker as a Measure of Progress

The index of output per worker is the quotient of indexes
of output and employment, and hence is heir to all the ob-
jections that can be raised against them. Indeed the index
of output per worker is likely to be more sensitive to errors
of measurement because opposite errors in the indexes of

[3]The expression, workers per unit of output, is used at this point in
preference to the alternative (and reciprocal) expression, output per
worker, because of graphical convenience.

quantity and employment are compounded: a 10 percent overstatement of output and a 10 percent understatement of employment will lead to a 22 percent overstatement of output per worker. Any disparity in the coverage of output and employment—and it is never possible to make them correspond exactly—is an additional source of error. But these are obvious limitations, and need not be elaborated.

A second type of qualification must be attached to short-run fluctuations in output per worker. Output per man-hour in the automobile industry fell 16.7 percent from 1929 to 1931, but surely this does not mean that more primitive techniques were used in the later year. The dates are a sufficient clue to the explanation: in many industries output will fluctuate more widely than employment because the entrepreneur cannot (for contractual, technical, or other reasons) make proportionate changes in his labor force. We should recognize also the difficulty of achieving comparability between output and employment in short periods; for example, the considerable fluctuations in goods in process during a cycle are not reflected in the usual measures of output. Short-run changes in output per worker cannot be interpreted as measures of economic progress.

The third type of qualification arises because we are comparing all output with only one input. If an entrepreneur substitutes other resources for labor because labor has become more expensive, and not because the other resources have become cheaper or improved, output per worker necessarily rises. Yet efficiency may have fallen, whether measured by the entrepreneur's costs or by social costs (of which something will be said presently). The phenomenon can be widespread: output per worker can be rising in every industry while national income is falling. This line of thought suggests that the index of output per worker will be more accurate as a measure of economic progress the greater the importance of labor in the industry. We examine the suggestion more closely below.

Patterns of Changes in Output per Worker

Indexes of output per worker are a relatively recent acquisition and their properties deserve much study. One of these properties is the pattern of changes in output among the various industries. Is there little or much dispersion in changes in output per worker among industries? Do industries maintain a fairly stable pattern or do their relative positions with respect to the growth of output per worker fluctuate widely? These and similar questions are pertinent to numerous current applications of the indexes. For example, it is often argued that wage rates should follow output per worker. But unless most firms (and therefore industries) have approximately equal changes in output per worker, this criterion may conflict with equality of wages within an occupation. Or again, if output per worker does not increase steadily, but fluctuates widely about its trend, the current procedures for forecasting income and employment require some revision.

The pattern of changes in output per worker may be glimpsed from data on thirty-two manufacturing industries for which Fabricant has presented continuous series back to 1899. The frequency distributions of percentage changes in output per worker per year have very wide spreads (Table 12).[4] The standard deviation of the percentage increases in output never fell below 3.2 percent and in half the periods equaled or exceeded 5 percent. There is no apparent tendency for dispersion to decline. The variation among all manufacturing industries was doubtless larger, for our restriction of manufacturing industries to those for which data were available for forty years excludes most new industries.

The effect of variation in working hours plays an uncertain part in this picture of diversity, hence comparable indexes were computed for 13 of the 32 industries for which

[4]The annual percentages are calculated by halving the biennial changes and taking a fifth of quintennial changes; use of compound interest formula would have reduced the scatter inappreciably.

TABLE 12

Frequency Distribution of Thirty-two Manufacturing Industries by Percentage Changes in Output per Worker per Year, 1899-1939

PERCENTAGE CHANGE IN OUTPUT PER WORKER	1899-1904	1904-09	1909-14	1914-19	1919-21	1921-23	1923-25	1925-27	1927-29	1929-31	1931-33	1933-35	1935-37	1937-39
−18 to −15					1				1	1				
−15 to −12											2	1		
−12 to −9											3	2		
−9 to −6				3	1						8	3		
−6 to −3		1	2		3	2	1		1	1	4	5	3	
−3 to 0	8	3	6	12	7	1	3	2	3	4	9	4	4	2
0 to 3	17	13	14	8	4	3	6	17	7	4	8	9	12	7
3 to 6	1	10	8	3	3	7	13	5	11	11		5	6	12
6 to 9	3	1	3	2	5	8	2	6	3	2		2	8	5
9 to 12	1				4	2	6	1	3				2	2
12 to 15	1	1		1	3	8	1		1	1	2			4
15 to 18		1			1	2	1		2			2		
18 to 21		1			1							1		
21 plus			1*											
Average	1.6	3.4	3.0	0.	4.2	8.0	5.4	3.1	4.0	−.8	−3.2	2.3	3.6	5.4
Standard deviation	3.8	5.0	6.6	4.2	7.6	5.4	4.3	3.2	6.2	7.0	3.6	7.4	3.5	4.3

*36.2

man-hours were known from 1929 to 1939. The comparison indicates, as one would expect, that output per man-hour rose more rapidly than output per worker except in the period when hours were lengthened, 1935-37 (see Table 13). But the picture of diversity persists; indeed the standard deviation of percentage changes in output per man-hour are larger in four of the five periods. It seems clear that the average change in labor productivity in a period is approached by relatively few industries.

TABLE 13

Annual Percentage Changes in Output per Worker and per Manhour, and Standard Deviations of these Changes Thirteen Manufacturing Industries, 1929-1939

	1929-31	1931-33	1933-35	1935-37	1937-39
% Change in Output per					
Worker	−.4	−1.6	3.2	2.7	5.2
Manhour	3.8	3.7	6.8	1.3	5.8
Standard Deviation of					
% Changes in Output per					
Worker	5.4	3.0	7.0	2.5	4.0
Manhour	5.2	3.5	7.7	3.1	4.6

Nor is there strong evidence of a stable pattern among the industries. If the 32 industries are ranked according to the percentage change in output per worker within each of the 14 periods for which data are available, one may test the existence of a stable pattern by an analysis of ranks.[5] This test does not reveal a systematic pattern; the probability of as large or a larger departure from a random distribution of ranks by industries under random sampling is one-tenth. In 13 of these industries for which output per man-hour is available since 1929, the test reveals no stability in the ranks of changes in either output per man-hour or output per man.[6]

If the indexes are accurate, we may conclude that increases in output per worker are not stable through time, either within or among individual manufacturing industries.

The Measurement of Changes in Efficiency

Since output per worker, useful though it be, is an incomplete measure of economic progress, can we go further and measure changes in the efficiency with which all resources are used? Efficiency is usually defined as

$$\frac{\text{Output}}{\text{Input of Labor} + \text{Input of Other Resources}},$$

where, for convenience, we shall call these other resources (materials, capital equipment, management, etc.) 'capital'. All the quantities are flows during an equal period—annual product, man-years, and annual services of capital. They must be measured in comparable physical units; in value terms the ratio of receipts to expenditures is (with certain definitions) unity.

But we are interested in changes in efficiency, not its abso-

[5]See Milton Friedman, 'The Use of Ranks to Avoid the Assumption of Normality Implicit in the Analysis of Variance', *Journal of the American Statistical Association*, Dec. 1937, pp. 675-701.
[6]The probabilities of as large or larger a departure from a random distribution of industrial ranks is almost .7 when the rankings are by either output per worker or per man-hour.

lute magnitude. We can measure changes in efficiency if, in addition to the indexes of output and employment we already possess, we can somehow find (1) the ratio of the quantity of capital services in one period to the quantity in another period, and (2) the ratio of the quantity of labor services to that of capital services in either period.[7]

The first requirement, the relative change in the flow of capital services in real terms, cannot be estimated at all precisely. The net book value of capital assets in current dollars has been estimated by Fabricant for 1904 and 1937 in the major manufacturing groups, but unfortunately he necessarily omits land and rented equipment, as well as management, which we lump with capital. Nor do we have any information on the extent to which the assets were used in the two years. Fabricant estimates that the appropriate price index to deflate the 1937 values to a 1904 base is about 180. This deflator registers only price changes, whereas we would like to take some account also of quality changes. Moreover, the index refers to all manufacturing, and the appropriate deflators for individual industry groups might vary considerably.

Serious difficulties are also encountered in seeking the ratio between labor and capital services. If we can invoke Marshall's principle of substitution—that the entrepreneur adjusts the quantities of various productive services so that at

[7]The ratio of efficiency in period 2 to efficiency in period 1 is given by

$$\frac{Q_2}{Q_1} \cdot \frac{C_1 + L_1}{C_2 + L_2} \, ,$$

where Q, C, and L represent quantities of output, capital, and labor respectively, and the subscripts refer to the two periods. This expression can be rewritten as

$$\frac{Q_2}{Q_1} \cdot \frac{\dfrac{C_1}{C_2}\dfrac{C_2}{L_2} + \dfrac{L_1}{L_2}}{\dfrac{C_2}{L_2} + 1} \, ,$$

whence it is clear that we need to know C_1/C_2 and C_2/L_2 (or, alternatively, C_1/L_1, as can be seen by dividing numerator and denominator of the first expression by L_1).

the margin he obtains equal product per dollar of expenditure on each—the ratio of payroll to other value-added is an estimate of the ratio of labor to capital.[8]

But Marshall's law pertains to competitive equilibrium, and our data refer to single years in which departures from equilibrium may have been large. Evidence offered below, however, suggests that the ratio of labor services to capital services is easier to estimate with tolerable accuracy than the relative change in capital in real terms between periods.

The changes in output per worker and output per unit of capital that one may construct along these lines are given in Table 14; efficiency of all inputs is the weighted average of these changes, using the 1937 ratio of value-added-other-than-wages to wages as the relative weight.[9] The ranks of the industries by gains in efficiency differ somewhat from those by increase in output per worker; the largest differences occur in petroleum and coal products, where a large increase in capital offsets a large increase in output per worker, and in leather products, where the reverse takes place.[10] The general correspondence between efficiency and output per worker is

[8]By the law of substitution, if MP_1 and MP_c are the marginal products of labor and capital respectively, and p_1 and p_c are their prices,

$$\frac{MP_1}{p_1} = \frac{MP_c}{p_c};$$

and if L and C are quantities of labor and capital respectively, the ratio of L to C in physical (product) terms is

$$\frac{L\,MP_1}{C\,MP_c} = \frac{Lp_1}{Cp_c}.$$

[9]The ratio of efficiency in period 2 to that in period 1 may be written,

$$\frac{1}{\frac{C_2}{L_2}+1}\left[\left(\frac{Q_2C_1}{Q_1C_2}\right)\frac{C_2}{L_2} + \left(\frac{Q_2L_1}{Q_1L_2}\right)\right].$$

The terms within parentheses are the ratio of output per unit of capital in period 2 to that in period 1 and the ratio of output per worker in period 2 to that in period 1. The weights are C_2/L_2 and 1.

[10]The rank correlation between changes in efficiency and output per worker is .74.

TABLE 14

Percentage Changes in Output per Worker, Output per Unit of Capital, and Efficiency in the Use of all Resources in Twelve Manufacturing Industries, 1904-1937

| | PERCENTAGE CHANGE | | |
| | OUTPUT PER | | |
	Worker	Unit of Capital	Efficiency
Transportation equipment	308	130	228
Tobacco products	445	100	175
Printing and publishing	156	142	147
Chemical products	147	119	126
Paper products	122	36	69
Beverages	44	75	69
Leather products	17	109	61
Textile products	42	73	57
Petroleum and coal products	239	−45	39
Iron and steel products	54	28	38
Food products	27	17	21
Forest products	6	−42	−18

due in part to the importance of labor (for wages vary from 20 to 50 percent of value-added) and in part to a weak association between changes in output per worker and output per unit of capital.[11]

Some check on the reliability of the 1937 estimate of the ratio of capital services to labor services is afforded by comparing it, and the resulting index of efficiency, with that computed from 1904 data. Because of changes in Census classification, the comparison can be made readily for only six industries (Table 15). The effects of shifting to the earlier

TABLE 15

Ratio of Capital to Labor and Percentage Change in Efficiency, 1904-1937, Based on 1904 and 1937 Value-Added Data
Six Manufacturing Industries

| | RATIO OF CAPITAL TO LABOR | | % CHANGE IN EFFICIENCY | |
	1904 Data	1937 Data	1904 Data	1937 Data
Tobacco products	2.25	3.64	150	175
Printing and publishing	2.23	2.37	147	147
Paper products	1.43	1.78	64	69
Leather products	1.03	.90	50	61
Petroleum and coal products	2.05	2.33	−24	39
Forest products	1.14	.99	−26	−18

11The rank correlation between changes in output per worker and output per unit of capital is .38.

ratio of capital to labor are small except in petroleum and coal products, where the index of efficiency is sensitive to the weight used to combine outputs per unit of labor and capital because of the great difference between their movements.

It cannot be claimed that these rough estimates of changes in efficiency have much more than illustrative value. Yet they should serve to remind us that it is important to measure all inputs of resources before we draw conclusions with respect to changes in efficiency. Even the present, very imperfect measures of changes in output per unit of capital give, I think, a more accurate picture of changes in efficiency than one could obtain from data on output per worker alone.

Where do the National Bureau studies of employment and output fit in the broad program of economic investigation? That program may be divided into three principal branches. The first has for its subject the contemporary structure and operations of the economic system; the second, the short term fluctuations in the level of activity of the system; and the third, the long term growth or decline of the economy and its parts. It is primarily in this third branch of economic development that the National Bureau studies we have been discussing fall.

The theory of economic development is concerned with the long term movements in (1) aggregate output and its composition; (2) the quantity, composition, and efficiency of use of resources; and (3) the distribution of income. These laconic rubrics conceal more than they reveal the variety of problems and findings in the theory of development. A brief elaboration of some of the material discussed in our survey of the productivity studies may provide a more informative, if less comprehensive, characterization. We shall give four examples.

1) It is a familiar and important datum of economic discussion that the output of commodities has risen rapidly relative to population, but the National Bureau studies provide us with much more precise measures of this development than were hitherto available. They indicate that output of commodities per head of population increased by three-quarters between 1899 and 1929, then fell sharply and did not fully recover, let alone approach an extrapolation of the previous upward trend, during the 'thirties. The increase in the proportion of the labor force in the service industries argues that the increase of commodities to 1929 was not obtained by producing fewer services. The substantial movement of activities and of labor from the household to the market supports this inference, for in all probability the output of services per

worker of given quality is higher in the market than within the household.

2) The persistent decline in the percentage rate of growth of individual industries is another finding of general significance. Established industries grow at a diminishing rate or actually decline, and the steady growth of aggregate output has been due in part to the rise of new industries, and not merely (as we might intuitively expect) to a canceling of increasing and decreasing rates of growth. This helps to explain the pessimistic bias of long-term forecasts. The great industries of the day are usually growing slowly or declining —each generation has its turnpikes, clippers, railroads, or trucks. New industries are necessarily small, and most never amount to much. Arithmetic tells us that aggregate output can grow at a steady pace despite these phenomena, but arithmetic is unheeded because it tells us that almost any movement of aggregate output is consistent with those of individual outputs. The studies of economic development are decidedly more informative.

3) If we look at the composition of output from the viewpoint of consumer wants rather than from the viewpoint of industries, we find further reason to distrust intuition. When John Stuart Mill contemplated the prospect of a stationary state he found less cause for concern than his predecessors had: if men could satisfy their stable need for bread with less effort, they could devote more attention to philosophy. Apparently this is not the whole choice; had it been, controversy might now be raging over the five-hour week. Mill's bread was really a sack of flour on the grocer's counter; it is now an enriched slice (baked by 1/250 of the labor force) suitably presented in a restaurant (employing 1/40 of the labor force). The workman has decided to work and earn beyond his basic wants, in part because he has additional wants and in part so his wife too can philosophize.

4) It is a commonplace of economic thinking that advanced industrial countries become nations of wage earners

employed by large industrial units. The tendency in this direction was indeed long and pronounced, but it has not maintained itself in recent decades. If we roughly classify as independent proprietors and employees of small scale enterprise the labor force in agriculture, the professions, trade, and personal services, the proportion declined from seven-tenths in 1870 to one-half in 1920, but has since risen slightly.* The intellectual father of modern capitalism described it as a nation of shopkeepers; he was wrong, for it was a nation of farmers. But should the service industries continue their rapid rate of growth, capitalism may yet develop a nation of shopkeepers.

In 1798 Thomas R. Malthus advanced the theory that the mass of mankind—in advanced countries—could live well only if the population did not tend to grow rapidly (which it did). This theory ruled almost unchallenged in economics for a quarter century and exerted strong influence for at least another quarter century. Yet it was wrong in at least some respects even in the early decades (population grew at a large, relatively constant geometrical rate in England), and it was wrong in all important respects by the middle of the century.

More recently the Malthusian theory has been almost exactly reversed in one version of the 'stagnation' theory: that the mass of mankind—in advanced countries characterized by free enterprise—can live well (under a moderate balanced budget) only if the population grows rapidly (which it won't). It is to be hoped that the stagnation theory will meet a better scientific fate than the Malthusian doctrine. We need not wait a generation or more to begin the task of accepting or rejecting an important theory on the basis of careful empirical tests. The studies reviewed in this essay should prove helpful in making these tests.

*Daniel Carson, *Industrial Composition of Manpower in the United States, 1870-1940* (unpublished report submitted to the Conference on Research in Income and Wealth, November 1946), Tables 1-2.

TABLE A
Indexes of Output in Six Industries, 1899-1940
(1929: 100)

	MANUFAC-TURING	AGRICUL-TURE	MINING	ELECTRIC LIGHT & POWER	GAS	STEAM RAILROADS*
1899	27.5	69.4	25.7		15.8	31
1900	28.0	70.1	27.8			35
1901	31.6	68.7	29.3		22.7	37
1902	35.4	71.5	30.6	3.6	21.4	40
1903	36.3	72.2	34.4		24.0	44
1904	34.1	75.7	35.5		25.6	45
1905	40.7	75.0	39.6		26.7	48
1906	43.7	81.9	41.1		29.8	54
1907	44.2	76.4	44.5	7.5	32.8	60
1908	36.5	77.8	41.6		34.8	56
1909	43.4	77.1	47.3		37.7	56
1910	46.2	79.2	50.1		39.8	65
1911	44.2	81.2	49.4		41.8	65
1912	50.8	85.4	53.0	13.0	46.6	67
1913	54.4	82.6	55.8	13.6	48.5	75
1914	51.1	89.6	51.9	15.2	51.1	72
1915	59.9	89.6	56.6	16.6	52.3	69
1916	71.2	82.6	65.3	21.1	58.8	82
1917	70.6	86.1	68.9	24.5	64.7	96
1918	69.8	90.3	69.4	31.4	63.8	99
1919	61.0	86.8	60.2	36.0	67.2	93
1920	66.5	90.3	69.7	39.3	69.0	102
1921	53.3	81.9	57.1	36.3	62.9	78
1922	68.4	90.3	61.4	41.2	67.9	83
1923	76.9	91.7	84.6	50.0	73.7	98
1924	73.1	95.1	79.7	54.9	76.5	92
1925	81.9	95.8	82.5	63.5	77.8	97
1926	86.8	101.4	89.5	73.5	85.8	102
1927	87.1	97.9	91.8	81.7	90.4	98
1928	91.2	102.1	91.8	89.5	93.8	98
1929	100.0	100.0	100.0	100.0	100.0	100
1930	85.4	100.7	88.2	103.5	101.4	86
1931	72.0	104.2	73.5	101.9	98.9	69
1932	54.1	100.0	59.1	92.7	92.5	52
1933	62.6	97.2	64.0	92.8	88.4	55
1934	69.2	83.3	69.7	99.2	92.0	60
1935	82.7	92.4	75.3	108.2	95.5	63
1936	97.0	93.1	88.4	123.4	100.0	76
1937	103.3	106.2	99.5	136.3	103.7	81
1938	81.0	105.6	85.1	136.8	101.1	66
1939	102.7	110.4	94.1	151.6	106.3	75
1940		110.6		167.7	115.3	

SOURCES: Manufacturing: Fabricant, *Employment in Manufacturing, 1899-1939*, p. 331.
Agriculture: Barger and Landsberg, *op. cit.*, p. 21.
Mining: Barger and Schurr, *op. cit.*, p. 14.
Electric Light and Power: Gould, *op. cit.*, p. 42.
Gas: *ibid.*, p. 103.
Railroads: Unpublished study by Barger.

*Year ending in June through 1916, thereafter year ending in December. Index for year ending December 1916 is 87.

TABLE B

Indexes of Employment in Six Industries, 1899-1940
(1929: 100)

	MANUFAC- TURING	AGRICUL- TURE (1930: 100)	MINING	ELECTRIC LIGHT & POWER	GAS	STEAM RAILROADS*
1899	53.5					55
1900	55.6	91.1				60
1901	58.3					63
1902	63.1		73.3	10.4	40.4	70
1903	65.2					78
1904	61.5					77
1905	68.4					82
1906	71.7					90
1907	74.9			16.3	53.9	99
1908	66.3					85
1909	74.3					89
1910	77.5	101.8				100
1911	77.5					99
1912	80.7			27.1	68.3	102
1913	81.3					109
1914	78.1					101
1915	81.8					92
1916	95.7					98
1917	102.1			36.1	77.4	106
1918	104.3			39.0		112
1919	100.5			41.1	79.4	116
1920	100.5	103.2		45.2		123
1921	77.0			46.8		101
1922	85.6			51.6		98
1923	97.9			66.9		112
1924	90.9			71.8		106
1925	93.6			73.6	91.7	105
1926	95.7			82.8		107
1927	93.6			85.9		105
1928	93.6			91.9		100
1929	100.0		100.0	100.0	100.0	100
1930	86.6	100.0		103.3	94.2	90
1931	73.3			96.1	89.4	76
1932	62.6			83.7	82.1	62
1933	69.0			78.5	85.6	59
1934	80.7			81.6	90.4	61
1935	85.6		58.8	83.7	91.3	60
1936	93.0		68.9	89.8	97.2	65
1937	102.1		71.9	96.3	97.4	68
1938	85.6		59.0	93.2	94.6	58
1939	94.1		60.6	92.7	95.3	60
1940		86.9		94.9	99.3	

SOURCES: Manufacturing: Same as Table A (wage earners only).
Agriculture: Barger and Landsberg, *op. cit.*, p. 246 (farmers and adult male laborers, 1940 figure added).
Mining: Barger and Schurr, *op. cit.*, p. 343. (Manhours, not strictly comparable with output index.)
Other: Same as Table A.

*Index for year ending December 1916 is 101.

TABLE C

Indexes of Employment per Unit of Output
in Six Industries, 1899-1940
(1929: 100)

	MANUFAC-TURING	AGRICUL-TURE (1930: 100)	MINING	ELECTRIC LIGHT & POWER	GAS	STEAM RAILROADS*
1899	196					175
1900	198	131				169
1901	184					172
1902	178		240	318	189	175
1903	182					179
1904	180					172
1905	171					170
1906	167					166
1907	171			240	164	166
1908	184					151
1909	173					158
1910	171	130				155
1911	176					152
1912	159			231	147	152
1913	151					146
1914	155					140
1915	137					133
1916	135					119
1917	145			162	120	111
1918	151			136		113
1919	165			125	118	124
1920	153	115		125		120
1921	145			139		130
1922	125			134		119
1923	127			141		114
1924	125			136		114
1925	116			119	118	108
1926	112			114		105
1927	108			105		106
1928	104			103		102
1929	100		100	100	100	100
1930	102	100		99.8	92.9	104
1931	102			94.3	90.4	110
1932	116			90.3	88.8	119
1933	112			84.5	96.8	107
1934	118			82.2	98.3	102
1935	104		78.1	77.3	95.6	96
1936	96		77.9	72.7	97.2	85
1937	100		72.3	70.6	93.9	84
1938	106		69.3	68.1	93.6	87
1939	92		64.4	61.1	89.7	81
1940		79		56.6	86.1	

SOURCE: Derived from Tables A and B.
*Index for year ending December 1916 is 116.

INDEX

National Bureau Publications
Still in Print

BOOKS

*Listed also as the first volume under Studies in Business Cycles.

II Studies in Consumer Instalment Financing

III Studies in Business Financing

1 Manufacturing Output, 1929-1937 (Dec. 1940)
Solomon Fabricant .25

3 Finished Commodities since 1879, Output and Its
Composition (Aug. 1941)
William H. Shaw .25

4 The Relation between Factory Employment and Output
since 1899 (Dec. 1941)
Solomon Fabricant .25

5 Railway Freight Traffic in Prosperity and Depression
(Feb. 1942) Thor Hultgren .25

6 Uses of National Income in Peace and War (March 1942)
Simon Kuznets .25

10 The Effect of War on Business Financing: Manufacturing
and Trade, World War I (Nov. 1943)
R. A. Young and C. H. Schmidt .50

11 The Effect of War on Currency and Deposits (Sept. 1943)
Charles R. Whittlesey .35

12 Prices in a War Economy: Some Aspects of the Present
Price Structure of the United States (Oct. 1943)
Frederick C. Mills .50

13 Railroad Travel and the State of Business (Dec. 1943)
Thor Hultgren .35

14 The Labor Force in Wartime America (March 1944)
Clarence D. Long .50

15 Railway Traffic Expansion and Use of Resources in World
War II (Feb. 1944)
Thor Hultgren .35

16 British and American Plans for International Currency
Stabilization (Jan. 1944)
J. H. Riddle .35

17 National Product, War and Prewar (Feb. 1944)
Simon Kuznets .50

18 Production of Industrial Materials in World Wars I and II
(March 1944)
Geoffrey H. Moore .50

19 Canada's Financial System in War (April 1944)
B. H. Higgins .50

20 Nazi War Finance and Banking (April 1944)
Otto Nathan .50

22 Bank Liquidity and the War (May 1945)
Charles R. Whittlesey .50

NATIONAL BUREAU OF ECONOMIC RESEARCH
1819 Broadway, New York 23, N. Y.